Spell Book Journal

A Diary for Wiccans, Witches, Pagans to Record
Spells, Rituals, Incantations, and Reflections

The Symbolism of the Moon Phases

New Moon (Dark Moon)

Fresh beginnings,
set goals for future,
planning, divination

Crescent Moon

Growth, thriving,
motivation,
and success

Waning Crescent

Getting rid of negative energy,
meditation, evaluation, working
on becoming better.

Waxing Crescent

Development, growth,
creative thinking,
and solution

First Quarter Moon

Decisions, actions,
creativity, conquering
the challenges

Last Quarter Moon

Spiritual healing,
letting go of past pain
and feelings, banishing,
and meditation

Gibbous Moon

Step back and look
closely in Your Life; what
are you doing right or wrong?
correction, adapting to your
current situation

Disseminating Moon

Be grateful, gratitude, appreciation,
hopefulness for the future

Balsamic Moon

Recovery and healing,
time to yield and repose,
stillness, being at peace

Full Moon

Power and purity,
celebration, be present,
and salutation

Calendar

January
Cold Moon

February
Quickening Moon

March
Storm Moon

April
Wind Moon

May
Flower Moon

June
Sun Moon

July
Blessing Moon

August
Corn Moon

September
Harvest Moon

October
Blood Moon

November
Mourning Moon

December
Long Nights Moon

Candles

White
Protection,
peace, purity,
and harmony

Black
Protection, banishing
negative energy,
banishing hexes,
and cleaning

Red
Lust, love,
strength,
and courage

Pink
Calmness, gentleness,
romantic love,
and compassion

Green
Money,
prosperity, success,
and health

Purple
Psychic power,
originality, creativity,
and spiritual
awareness

Orange
Vitality, enthusiasm,
excitement, happiness,
and optimism

Blue
Communication,
connection, healing,
calming, and relaxation

Gold
Wealth, prosperity,
money, and connection
to the gods (Prestige & Charm)

Brown
Homeliness, comfort,
security, communicating and
dealing with animals

Yellow
Intelligence,
learning, focus
and logic

Wheel of The Year

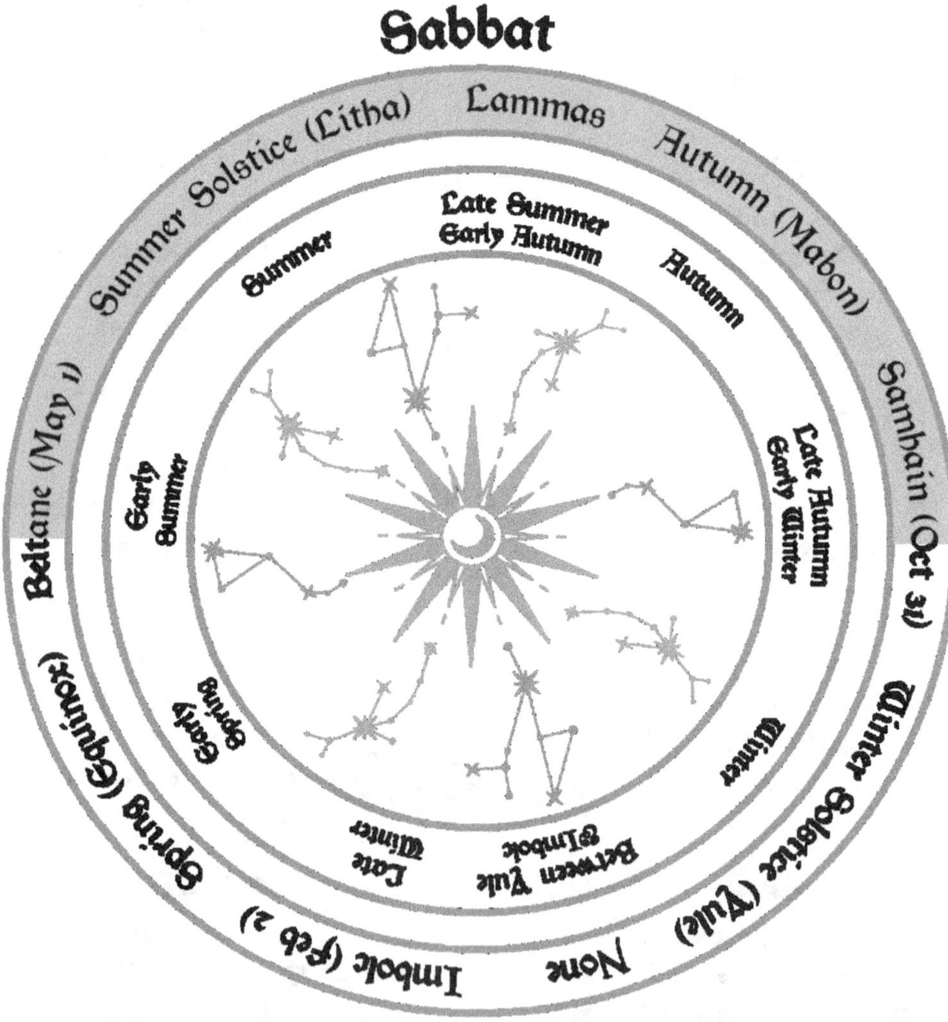

Sabbat

Beltane (May 1)

Summer Solstice (Litha)

Lammas

Autumn (Mabon)

Samhain (Oct 31)

Winter Solstice (Yule)

None

Imbolc (Feb 2)

Spring (Equinox)

Summer

Late Summer
Early Autumn

Autumn

Late Autumn
Early Winter

Winter

Between Yule
& Imbolc

Late
Winter

Early
Spring

Early
Summer

Crystals Meanings

Agate
Connected to Earth element and matters of the mind, energy, and loneliness

Amethyst
Connected with the Water element, healing, rituals, depression, and anxiety

Bloodstone
Connected to the Fire Element, healing, prosperity, and fertility

Calcite
Connected to the Water element, grounding, healing, joy, and purification

Diamond
Connected to the Air and Fire Element, marriage, impotence, intuition, and meditation

Emerald
Connected to the Goddess, Taurus, visualization, and protection of children

Fluorite
Connected to the Air and Water Elements, Zodiac, clarity, and crystal healing

Garnet
Connected to the Fire element, moon magic, reproductive disorders, and balance

Jade
Connected to the Earth element, truthfulness, serenity, and healing

Malachite
Connected the Earth and Water elements, powerful magic, transformation, and warnings

Note: To check your crystal's energy, you close your eyes and feel its energy. Clean your crystals by soaking in spring water, wash in rainwater, smudge, buried in sand, sunlight, and moonlight.

Crystals Meanings

Obsidian

Connected to the fire element, antitoxin, intuitiveness, and scrying

Pearl

Connected to the Water element and the moon, Gemini, good and bad luck

Ruby

Connected to the fire element, creativity, generosity, and wisdom

Sapphire

Connected to the Moon and Saturn, healing, inner peace, and inspiration

Tourmaline

Connected to the Water element, personal power, decision making, and rational thinking

Tiger's Eye

Helps you for building courage, confidence and stay centered.

Moonstone

A goddess stone helps you bring about fresh beginnings.

Clear Quartz

Excellent healing power, get rid of negative energy and give clarity.

Aventurine

Connected to the Earth and nature, prosperity, luck, and opportunity

Rose Quartz

Love, compassion and helps you for healing hurt and pain

Note: To check your crystal's energy, you close your eyes and feel its energy. Clean your crystals by soaking in spring water, wash in rainwater, smudge, buried in sand, sunlight, and moonlight.

Zodiac
Signs Meanings

Capricorn

Magic Related to

Responsibility, healing, and ambition

Sagittarius

Magic Related to

Generosity and optimism

Scorpio

Magic Related to

Divination, renewal, and banishing

Libra

Magic Related to

Harmony, peace, and love

Virgo

Magic Related to

Health and healing

Leo

Magic Related to

Self-confidence and self-expression

Cancer

Magic Related to

Home and family

Gemini

Magic Related to

Communication, intelligence, and adaptability

Taurus

Magic Related to

Self-esteem, love, money, and prosperity

Aries

Magic Related to

Self-improvement, vitality, and health

Pisces

Magic Related to

Spirituality, charity, and self-reflection

Aquarius

Magic Related to

Friendship and acquaintances

Numerology
Meanings

Eternity

0

Infinity

Beginnings

1

Creation

Balance

2

Intuition

Creativity

3

Self-expression

Foundation

4

Hard Working

Change

5

Challenge

Harmony

6

Love

Spirituality

7

Prosperity

Manifestation

8

Divination

Wisdom

9

Knowledge

Witchcraft Magical Tools:

 **Athame**

Represents the element Fire, energy cutting and directing magical power, casting a circle, charging objects with energy and symbol of the God

 **Bell**

Represents the Goddess, used for invocation, banishment, and drive away negativity from a circle, signal the beginning of a rite, disperse the energy after the spell

 **Boline**

Cutting objects in the earthly plane, cutting tools, practical knife

 **Cauldron**

Symbolic of the three aspects the Goddess, womb, ceremonial fires, scrying, holding ingredients, and burning items

 Chalice

Represents the womb, holds a drink for ritual purposes, wine, water, and libations

 **Pentacle**

Represents the element Earth, summons specific energies or spirits, the centerpiece of an altar

 **Wand**

Made from sacred wood and carved or decorated with personal items as crystals and gems

 **Book of Shadow**

A personal collection of magical experiences, a written account of rituals, spells, herbal remedies, or other information

Herbs Meanings

Allspice
(Magical Properties)
Healing, luck, money, and energy

Basil
(Magical Properties)
Wealth, love, sympathy, and protection

Cinnamon
(Magical Properties)
Power, spirituality, healing, and strength

Dill
(Magical Properties)
Money, lust, luck, and protection

Ginger
(Magical Properties)
Confidence, sensuality, prosperity, and success

Mint
(Magical Properties)
Wealth, healing, vitality, and communication

Nutmeg
(Magical Properties)
Bringing luck, protection, prosperity, and banishing hexes

Parsley
(Magical Properties)
Fertility, well-being, anxiety, and quick recovery from sickness

Allspice
(Magical Properties)
Healing, luck, money, and energy

Allspice
(Magical Properties)
Healing, luck, money, and energy

Sage
(Magical Properties)
Self-purification, spirituality, healing, spells, and wisdom

Rosemary
(Magical Properties)
Protection, royalty, purification, and healing

Lavender
(Magical Properties)
Peace, spirituality, love, and healing

Basil
(Magical Properties)
Wealth, love, sympathy, and protection

Date / Day of Week / Time

· · · · · ● **Name of spell/ritual** ● · · · · ·

_____

Statement of intention _____

_____

Moon Lunar Phase _____

Astrology/Planetary influences _____

_____

Weather _____

Materials or tools used/Ingredient/ Equipment

_____

_____

_____

Symbols used _____

Instructions _____

_____

Effective and feeling _____

_____

Immediate Changes and results _____

_____

Later changes and results _____

_____

Spell/Ritual rating _____

_____

_____

Date / Day of Week / Time

· · · · ● ● **Name of spell/ritual** ● ● · · · ·

_____

Statement of intention _____

_____

Moon Lunar Phase _____

Astrology/Planetary influences _____

_____

Weather _____

Materials or tools used/Ingredient/ Equipment

_____

_____

_____

Symbols used _____

Instructions _____

_____

Effective and feeling _____

_____

Immediate Changes and results _____

_____

Later changes and results _____

_____

Spell/Ritual rating _____

_____

_____

Date / Day of Week / Time

● ● ● ● ● **Name of spell/ritual** ● ● ● ● ● ●

_____

Statement of intention _____

_____

Moon Lunar Phase _____

Astrology/Planetary influences _____

_____

Weather _____

Materials or tools used/Ingredient/ Equipment

_____

_____

_____

Symbols used _____

Instructions _____

_____

Effective and feeling _____

_____

Immediate Changes and results _____

_____

Later changes and results _____

_____

Spell/Ritual rating _____

_____

_____

Date / Day of Week / Time

● ● ● ● ● ● **Name of spell/ritual** ● ● ● ● ● ●

_____

Statement of intention _____

_____

Moon Lunar P-hase _____

Astrology/Planetary influences _____

_____

Weather _____

Materials or tools used/Ingredient/ Equipment

_____
_____
_____

Symbols used _____

Instructions _____

_____

Effective and feeling _____

Immediate Changes and results _____

_____

Later changes and results _____

_____

Spell/Ritual rating _____

_____

_____

Date / Day of Week / Time

. . . . . ● **Name of spell/ritual** ● ● . . . . .

_____

Statement of intention _____

_____

Moon Lunar P-hase _____

Astrology/Planetary influences _____

_____

Weather _____

Materials or tools used/Ingredient/ Equipment

_____

_____

_____

Symbols used _____

Instructions _____

_____

Effective and feeling _____

_____

Immediate Changes and results _____

_____

Later changes and results _____

_____

Spell/Ritual rating _____

_____

_____

Date / Day of Week / Time

· · · · ● ● **Name of spell/ritual** ● ● · · · · ·

_____

Statement of intention _____

_____

Moon Lunar Phase _____

Astrology/Planetary influences _____

_____

Weather _____

Materials or tools used/Ingredient/ Equipment

_____

_____

_____

Symbols used _____

Instructions _____

_____

Effective and feeling _____

_____

Immediate Changes and results _____

_____

Later changes and results _____

_____

Spell/Ritual rating _____

_____

Date / Day of Week / Time

· · · · ● ● **Name of spell/ritual** ● ● · · · ·

_____

Statement of intention _____

_____

Moon Lunar P-hase _____

Astrology/Planetary influences _____

_____

Weather _____

Materials or tools used/Ingredient/ Equipment

_____

_____

_____

Symbols used _____

Instructions _____

_____

Effective and feeling _____

_____

Immediate Changes and results _____

_____

Later changes and results _____

_____

Spell/Ritual rating _____

_____

_____

Date / Day of Week / Time

· · · · · ● ● **Name of spell/ritual** ● ● · · · · ·

_____

Statement of intention _____

_____

Moon Lunar Phase _____

Astrology/Planetary influences _____

_____

Weather _____

Materials or tools used/Ingredient/ Equipment

_____
_____
_____

Symbols used _____
Instructions _____

_____

Effective and feeling _____

_____

Immediate Changes and results _____

_____

Later changes and results _____

_____

Spell/Ritual rating _____

_____

_____

Date / Day of Week / Time

• • • • • • Name of spell/ritual • • • • • •

_____

Statement of intention _____

_____

Moon Lunar Phase _____

Astrology/Planetary influences _____

_____

Weather _____

Materials or tools used/Ingredient/ Equipment

_____

_____

_____

Symbols used _____

Instructions _____

_____

Effective and feeling _____

Immediate Changes and results _____

_____

Later changes and results _____

_____

Spell/Ritual rating _____

_____

_____

Date / Day of Week / Time

· · · · ● ● ● **Name of spell/ritual** ● ● ● · · · ·

_____

Statement of intention _____

_____

Moon Lunar P-hase _____

Astrology/Planetary influences _____

_____

Weather _____

Materials or tools used/Ingredient/ Equipment

_____
_____
_____

Symbols used _____

Instructions _____

_____

Effective and feeling _____

_____

Immediate Changes and results _____

_____

Later changes and results _____

_____

Spell/Ritual rating _____

_____

_____

Date / Day of Week / Time

· · · · · ● Name of spell/ritual ● ● · · · · ·

_____

Statement of intention _____

_____

Moon Lunar P-hase _____

Astrology/Planetary influences _____

_____

Weather _____

Materials or tools used/Ingredient/ Equipment

_____

_____

_____

Symbols used _____

Instructions _____

_____

Effective and feeling _____

_____

Immediate Changes and results _____

_____

Later changes and results _____

_____

Spell/Ritual rating _____

_____

_____

Date / Day of Week / Time

· · · · ● ● **Name of spell/ritual** ● ● · · · · ·

_____

Statement of intention _____

_____

Moon Lunar P-base _____

Astrology/Planetary influences _____

_____

Weather _____

Materials or tools used/Ingredient/ Equipment

_____
_____
_____

Symbols used _____
Instructions _____

_____

Effective and feeling _____

_____

Immediate Changes and results _____

_____

Later changes and results _____

_____

Spell/Ritual rating _____

_____

_____

Date / Day of Week / Time

· · · · · ● **Name of spell/ritual** ● · · · · ·

_____

Statement of intention _____

_____

Moon Lunar P-hase _____

Astrology/Planetary influences _____

_____

Weather _____

Materials or tools used/Ingredient/ Equipment

_____

_____

_____

Symbols used _____

Instructions _____

_____

Effective and feeling _____

_____

Immediate Changes and results _____

_____

Later changes and results _____

_____

Spell/Ritual rating _____

_____

_____

Date / Day of Week / Time

· · · · ● ● **Name of spell/ritual** ● ● · · · ·

_____

Statement of intention _____

_____

Moon Lunar P-hase _____

Astrology/Planetary influences _____

_____

Weather _____

Materials or tools used/Ingredient/ Equipment

_____
_____
_____

Symbols used _____
Instructions _____

_____

Effective and feeling _____

_____

Immediate Changes and results _____

_____

Later changes and results _____

_____

Spell/Ritual rating _____

_____

_____

Date / Day of Week / Time

• • • • ● Name of spell/ritual ● • • • • •

_____

Statement of intention _____

_____

Moon Lunar P-hase _____

Astrology/Planetary influences _____

_____

Weather _____

Materials or tools used/Ingredient/ Equipment

_____

_____

_____

Symbols used _____

Instructions _____

_____

Effective and feeling _____

Immediate Changes and results _____

_____

Later changes and results _____

_____

Spell/Ritual rating _____

_____

_____

Date / Day of Week / Time

· · · ● ● ● **Name of spell/ritual** ● ● ● · · ·

_____

Statement of intention _____

_____

Moon Lunar Phase _____

Astrology/Planetary influences _____

_____

Weather _____

Materials or tools used/Ingredient/ Equipment

_____
_____
_____

Symbols used _____

Instructions _____

_____

Effective and feeling _____

_____

Immediate Changes and results _____

_____

Later changes and results _____

_____

Spell/Ritual rating _____

_____

_____

Date / Day of Week / Time

· · · · · ● **Name of spell/ritual** ● ● · · · · ·

_____

Statement of intention _____

_____

Moon Lunar P-hase _____

Astrology/Planetary influences _____

_____

Weather _____

Materials or tools used/Ingredient/ Equipment

_____
_____
_____

Symbols used _____

Instructions _____

_____

Effective and feeling _____

_____

Immediate Changes and results _____

_____

Later changes and results _____

_____

Spell/Ritual rating _____

_____

_____

Date / Day of Week / Time

• • • • • Name of spell/ritual • • • • •

_____

Statement of intention _____

_____

Moon Lunar P-hase _____

Astrology/Planetary influences _____

_____

Weather _____

Materials or tools used/Ingredient/ Equipment

_____

_____

_____

Symbols used _____

Instructions _____

_____

Effective and feeling _____

_____

Immediate Changes and results _____

_____

Later changes and results _____

_____

Spell/Ritual rating _____

_____

_____

Date ___ / Day of Week ___ / Time ___

• • • • • Name of spell/ritual • • • • •

_____

Statement of intention _____

_____

Moon Lunar P-hase _____

Astrology/Planetary influences _____

_____

Weather _____

Materials or tools used/Ingredient/ Equipment

_____

_____

_____

Symbols used _____

Instructions _____

_____

Effective and feeling _____

_____

Immediate Changes and results _____

_____

Later changes and results _____

_____

Spell/Ritual rating _____

_____

_____

Date / Day of Week / Time

· · · ● ● ● Name of spell/ritual ● ● ● · · ·

_____

Statement of intention _____

_____

Moon Lunar P-hase _____

Astrology/Planetary influences _____

_____

Weather _____

Materials or tools used/Ingredient/ Equipment

_____
_____
_____

Symbols used _____

Instructions _____

_____

Effective and feeling _____

_____

Immediate Changes and results _____

_____

Later changes and results _____

_____

Spell/Ritual rating _____

_____

_____

Date / Day of Week / Time

• • • • • Name of spell/ritual • • • • • •

_____

Statement of intention _____

_____

Moon Lunar P-hase _____

Astrology/Planetary influences _____

_____

Weather _____

Materials or tools used/Ingredient/ Equipment

_____
_____
_____

Symbols used _____

Instructions _____

_____

Effective and feeling _____

_____

Immediate Changes and results _____

_____

Later changes and results _____

_____

Spell/Ritual rating _____

_____

_____

Date / Day of Week / Time

• • • • • Name of spell/ritual • • • • •

_____

Statement of intention _____

_____

Moon Lunar P-hase _____

Astrology/Planetary influences _____

_____

Weather _____

Materials or tools used/Ingredient/ Equipment

_____
_____
_____

Symbols used _____

Instructions _____

_____

Effective and feeling _____

_____

Immediate Changes and results _____

_____

Later changes and results _____

_____

Spell/Ritual rating _____

_____

Date / Day of Week / Time

••••• **Name of spell/ritual** •••••

_____

Statement of intention _____

_____

Moon Lunar P–hase _____

Astrology/Planetary influences _____

_____

Weather _____

Materials or tools used/Ingredient/ Equipment

_____

_____

_____

Symbols used _____

Instructions _____

_____

Effective and feeling _____

_____

Immediate Changes and results _____

_____

Later changes and results _____

_____

Spell/Ritual rating _____

_____

_____

Date / Day of Week / Time

·····● Name of spell/ritual ●·····

_____

Statement of intention _____

_____

Moon Lunar P-hase _____

Astrology/Planetary influences _____

_____

Weather _____

Materials or tools used/Ingredient/ Equipment

_____
_____
_____

Symbols used _____

Instructions _____

_____

Effective and feeling _____

Immediate Changes and results _____

_____

Later changes and results _____

_____

Spell/Ritual rating _____

_____

_____

Date / Day of Week / Time

· · · · ● ● **Name of spell/ritual** ● ● ● · · · ·

_____

Statement of intention _____

_____

Moon Lunar P-hase _____

Astrology/Planetary influences _____

_____

Weather _____

Materials or tools used/Ingredient/ Equipment

_____
_____
_____

Symbols used _____

Instructions _____

_____

Effective and feeling _____

_____

Immediate Changes and results _____

_____

Later changes and results _____

_____

Spell/Ritual rating _____

_____

_____

Date / Day of Week / Time

· · · • • • Name of spell/ritual • • • · · ·

_____

Statement of intention _____

_____

Moon Lunar P-hase _____

Astrology/Planetary influences _____

_____

Weather _____

Materials or tools used/Ingredient/ Equipment

_____

_____

_____

Symbols used _____

Instructions _____

_____

Effective and feeling _____

_____

Immediate Changes and results _____

_____

Later changes and results _____

_____

Spell/Ritual rating _____

_____

_____

Date / Day of Week / Time

······ **Name of spell/ritual** ······

_____

Statement of intention _____

_____

Moon Lunar Phase _____

Astrology/Planetary influences _____

Weather _____

Materials or tools used/Ingredient/ Equipment

_____

_____

_____

Symbols used _____

Instructions _____

_____

Effective and feeling _____

_____

Immediate Changes and results _____

_____

Later changes and results _____

_____

Spell/Ritual rating _____

_____

_____

Date / Day of Week / Time

· · · · · ● **Name of spell/ritual** ● · · · · ·

_____

Statement of intention _____

_____

Moon Lunar P-base _____

Astrology/Planetary influences _____

_____

Weather _____

Materials or tools used/Ingredient/ Equipment

_____
_____
_____

Symbols used _____

Instructions _____

_____

Effective and feeling _____

_____

Immediate Changes and results _____

_____

Later changes and results _____

_____

Spell/Ritual rating _____

_____

_____

Date / Day of Week / Time

. . . . ● ● **Name of spell/ritual** ● ● . . . . .

_____

Statement of intention _____

_____

Moon Lunar P-hase _____

Astrology/Planetary influences _____

_____

Weather _____

Materials or tools used/Ingredient/ Equipment

_____

_____

_____

Symbols used _____

Instructions _____

_____

Effective and feeling _____

Immediate Changes and results _____

_____

Later changes and results _____

_____

Spell/Ritual rating _____

_____

_____

Date / Day of Week / Time

· · · ● ● ● Name of spell/ritual ● ● ● · · ·

_____

Statement of intention _____

_____

Moon Lunar P-hase _____

Astrology/Planetary influences _____

_____

Weather _____

Materials or tools used/Ingredient/ Equipment

_____
_____
_____

Symbols used _____

Instructions _____

_____

Effective and feeling _____

_____

Immediate Changes and results _____

_____

Later changes and results _____

_____

Spell/Ritual rating _____

_____

Date / Day of Week / Time

· · · · · ● **Name of spell/ritual** ● · · · · ·

_____

Statement of intention _____

_____

Moon Lunar P-hase _____

Astrology/Planetary influences _____

_____

Weather _____

Materials or tools used/Ingredient/ Equipment

_____
_____
_____

Symbols used _____

Instructions _____

_____

Effective and feeling _____

Immediate Changes and results _____

_____

Later changes and results _____

_____

Spell/Ritual rating _____

_____

_____

Date / Day of Week / Time

·······● **Name of spell/ritual** ●······

Statement of intention _____

_____

Moon Lunar Phase _____

Astrology/Planetary influences _____

Weather _____

Materials or tools used/Ingredient/ Equipment

_____

_____

_____

Symbols used _____

Instructions _____

_____

Effective and feeling _____

Immediate Changes and results _____

Later changes and results _____

Spell/Ritual rating _____

_____

Date / Day of Week / Time

- - - - • ● **Name of spell/ritual** ● ● • - - - -

_____

Statement of intention _____

_____

Moon Lunar P-hase _____

Astrology/Planetary influences _____

_____

Weather _____

Materials or tools used/Ingredient/ Equipment

_____
_____
_____

Symbols used _____

Instructions _____

_____

Effective and feeling _____

_____

Immediate Changes and results _____

_____

Later changes and results _____

_____

Spell/Ritual rating _____

_____

_____

Date / Day of Week / Time

• • • • • Name of spell/ritual • • • • • •

_____

Statement of intention _____

_____

Moon Lunar P-hase _____

Astrology/Planetary influences _____

_____

Weather _____

Materials or tools used/Ingredient/ Equipment

_____

_____

_____

Symbols used _____

Instructions _____

_____

Effective and feeling _____

_____

Immediate Changes and results _____

_____

Later changes and results _____

_____

Spell/Ritual rating _____

_____

_____

Date / Day of Week / Time

• • • • • Name of spell/ritual • • • • • •

_____

Statement of intention _____

_____

Moon Lunar P-hase _____

Astrology/Planetary influences _____

_____

Weather _____

Materials or tools used/Ingredient/ Equipment

_____

_____

_____

Symbols used _____

Instructions _____

_____

Effective and feeling _____

_____

Immediate Changes and results _____

_____

Later changes and results _____

_____

Spell/Ritual rating _____

_____

_____

Date / Day of Week / Time

• • • • • Name of spell/ritual • • • • • •

_____

Statement of intention _____

_____

Moon Lunar P-hase _____

Astrology/Planetary influences _____

_____

Weather _____

Materials or tools used/Ingredient/ Equipment

_____
_____
_____

Symbols used _____
Instructions _____

_____

Effective and feeling _____

_____

Immediate Changes and results _____

_____

Later changes and results _____

_____

Spell/Ritual rating _____

_____

_____

Date / Day of Week / Time

• • • • • Name of spell/ritual • • • • • •

_____

Statement of intention _____

_____

Moon Lunar P-hase _____

Astrology/Planetary influences _____

_____

Weather _____

Materials or tools used/Ingredient/ Equipment

_____
_____
_____

Symbols used _____

Instructions _____

_____

Effective and feeling _____

_____

Immediate Changes and results _____

_____

Later changes and results _____

_____

Spell/Ritual rating _____

_____

_____

Date / Day of Week / Time

● ● ● ● ● **Name of spell/ritual** ● ● ● ● ● ●

_____

Statement of intention _____

_____

Moon Lunar Phase _____

Astrology/Planetary influences _____

_____

Weather _____

Materials or tools used/Ingredient/ Equipment

_____
_____
_____

Symbols used _____

Instructions _____

_____

Effective and feeling _____

_____

Immediate Changes and results _____

_____

Later changes and results _____

_____

Spell/Ritual rating _____

_____

Date / Day of Week / Time

· · · · · ● **Name of spell/ritual** ● ● · · · · ·

_____

Statement of intention _____

_____

Moon Lunar Phase _____

Astrology/Planetary influences _____

_____

Weather _____

Materials or tools used/Ingredient/ Equipment

_____

_____

_____

Symbols used _____

Instructions _____

_____

Effective and feeling _____

_____

Immediate Changes and results _____

_____

Later changes and results _____

_____

Spell/Ritual rating _____

_____

_____

Date / Day of Week / Time

· · · • • • **Name of spell/ritual** • • • · · ·

_____

Statement of intention _____

_____

Moon Lunar P-hase _____

Astrology/Planetary influences _____

_____

Weather _____

Materials or tools used/Ingredient/ Equipment

_____

_____

_____

Symbols used _____

Instructions _____

_____

Effective and feeling _____

_____

Immediate Changes and results _____

_____

Later changes and results _____

_____

Spell/Ritual rating _____

_____

_____

Date / Day of Week / Time

· · · · · · Name of spell/ritual · · · · · ·

_____

Statement of intention _____

_____

Moon Lunar P-hase _____

Astrology/Planetary influences _____

_____

Weather _____

Materials or tools used/Ingredient/ Equipment

_____

_____

_____

Symbols used _____

Instructions _____

_____

Effective and feeling _____

_____

Immediate Changes and results _____

_____

Later changes and results _____

_____

Spell/Ritual rating _____

_____

_____

Date / Day of Week / Time

• • • • • **Name of spell/ritual** • • • • • •

Statement of intention _____

_____

Moon Lunar P-hase _____

Astrology/Planetary influences _____

_____

Weather _____

Materials or tools used/Ingredient/ Equipment

_____

_____

_____

Symbols used _____

Instructions _____

_____

Effective and feeling _____

_____

Immediate Changes and results _____

_____

Later changes and results _____

_____

Spell/Ritual rating _____

_____

_____

Date / Day of Week / Time

· · · · · · Name of spell/ritual · · · · · ·

_____

Statement of intention _____

_____

Moon Lunar P-hase _____

Astrology/Planetary influences _____

_____

Weather _____

Materials or tools used/Ingredient/ Equipment

_____

_____

Symbols used _____

Instructions _____

_____

Effective and feeling _____

_____

Immediate Changes and results _____

_____

Later changes and results _____

_____

Spell/Ritual rating _____

_____

_____

Date / Day of Week / Time

• • • • • Name of spell/ritual • • • • •

_____

Statement of intention _____

_____

Moon Lunar P-hase _____

Astrology/Planetary influences _____

_____

Weather _____

Materials or tools used/Ingredient/ Equipment

_____
_____
_____

Symbols used _____

Instructions _____

_____

Effective and feeling _____

_____

Immediate Changes and results _____

_____

Later changes and results _____

_____

Spell/Ritual rating _____

_____

_____

Date / Day of Week / Time

• • • • • Name of spell/ritual • • • • • •

_____

Statement of intention _____

_____

Moon Lunar P-hase _____

Astrology/Planetary influences _____

_____

Weather _____

Materials or tools used/Ingredient/ Equipment

_____

_____

_____

Symbols used _____

Instructions _____

_____

Effective and feeling _____

_____

Immediate Changes and results _____

_____

Later changes and results _____

_____

Spell/Ritual rating _____

_____

_____

Date / Day of Week / Time

• • • • • Name of spell/ritual • • • • •

_____

Statement of intention _____

_____

Moon Lunar P-hase _____

Astrology/Planetary influences _____

_____

Weather _____

Materials or tools used/Ingredient/ Equipment

_____

_____

_____

Symbols used _____

Instructions _____

_____

Effective and feeling _____

_____

Immediate Changes and results _____

_____

Later changes and results _____

_____

Spell/Ritual rating _____

_____

_____

Date / Day of Week / Time

· · · · · ● **Name of spell/ritual** ● · · · · ·

_____

Statement of intention _____

_____

Moon Lunar P-hase _____

Astrology/Planetary influences _____

_____

Weather _____

Materials or tools used/Ingredient/ Equipment

_____
_____
_____

Symbols used _____
Instructions _____

_____

Effective and feeling _____

_____

Immediate Changes and results _____

_____

Later changes and results _____

_____

Spell/Ritual rating _____

_____
_____

Date / Day of Week / Time

● ● ● ● ● Name of spell/ritual ● ● ● ● ● ●

_____

Statement of intention _____

_____

Moon Lunar P-hase _____

Astrology/Planetary influences _____

_____

Weather _____

Materials or tools used/Ingredient/ Equipment

_____
_____
_____

Symbols used _____

Instructions _____

_____

Effective and feeling _____

Immediate Changes and results _____

_____

Later changes and results _____

_____

Spell/Ritual rating _____

_____

_____

Date / Day of Week / Time

· · · · ● ● **Name of spell/ritual** ● ● · · · · ·

_____

Statement of intention _____

_____

Moon Lunar P-hase _____

Astrology/Planetary influences _____

_____

Weather _____

Materials or tools used/Ingredient/ Equipment

_____
_____
_____

Symbols used _____

Instructions _____

_____

Effective and feeling _____

_____

Immediate Changes and results _____

_____

Later changes and results _____

_____

Spell/Ritual rating _____

_____

_____

Date / Day of Week / Time

•••••• Name of spell/ritual ••••••

_____

Statement of intention   _____

_____

Moon Lunar Phase   _____

Astrology/Planetary influences   _____

_____

Weather   _____

Materials or tools used/Ingredient/ Equipment

_____
_____
_____

Symbols used   _____

Instructions   _____

_____

Effective and feeling   _____

_____

Immediate Changes and results   _____

_____

Later changes and results   _____

_____

Spell/Ritual rating   _____

_____

_____

Date / Day of Week / Time

• • • • • Name of spell/ritual • • • • •

_____

Statement of intention _____

_____

Moon Lunar P-hase _____

Astrology/Planetary influences _____

_____

Weather _____

Materials or tools used/Ingredient/ Equipment

_____

_____

_____

Symbols used _____

Instructions _____

_____

Effective and feeling _____

_____

Immediate Changes and results _____

_____

Later changes and results _____

_____

Spell/Ritual rating _____

_____

_____

Date / Day of Week / Time

● ● ● ● Name of spell/ritual ● ● ● ● ●

_____

Statement of intention _____

_____

Moon Lunar P-hase _____

Astrology/Planetary influences _____

_____

Weather _____

Materials or tools used/Ingredient/ Equipment

_____
_____
_____

Symbols used _____

Instructions _____

_____

Effective and feeling _____

_____

Immediate Changes and results _____

_____

Later changes and results _____

_____

Spell/Ritual rating _____

_____

_____

Date / Day of Week / Time

· · · · · ● **Name of spell/ritual** ● · · · · ·

_____

Statement of intention _____

_____

Moon Lunar P-hase _____

Astrology/Planetary influences _____

_____

Weather _____

Materials or tools used/Ingredient/ Equipment

_____

_____

_____

Symbols used _____

Instructions _____

_____

Effective and feeling _____

_____

Immediate Changes and results _____

_____

Later changes and results _____

_____

Spell/Ritual rating _____

_____

_____

Date / Day of Week / Time

• • • • ● **Name of spell/ritual** ● • • • • •

_____

Statement of intention _____

_____

Moon Lunar P-hase _____

Astrology/Planetary influences _____

_____

Weather _____

Materials or tools used/Ingredient/ Equipment

_____

_____

_____

Symbols used _____

Instructions _____

_____

Effective and feeling _____

Immediate Changes and results _____

_____

Later changes and results _____

_____

Spell/Ritual rating _____

_____

_____

Date / Day of Week / Time

• • • • ● Name of spell/ritual ● • • • • •

_____

Statement of intention _____

_____

Moon Lunar P-hase _____

Astrology/Planetary influences _____

_____

Weather _____

Materials or tools used/Ingredient/ Equipment

_____
_____
_____

Symbols used _____

Instructions _____

_____

Effective and feeling _____

_____

Immediate Changes and results _____

_____

Later changes and results _____

_____

Spell/Ritual rating _____

_____

_____

Date / Day of Week / Time

● ● ● ● ● ● Name of spell/ritual ● ● ● ● ● ●

_____

Statement of intention _____

_____

Moon Lunar P-hase _____

Astrology/Planetary influences _____

_____

Weather _____

Materials or tools used/Ingredient/ Equipment

_____
_____
_____

Symbols used _____
Instructions _____

_____

Effective and feeling _____

_____

Immediate Changes and results _____

_____

Later changes and results _____

_____

Spell/Ritual rating _____

_____

_____

Date / Day of Week / Time

······● **Name of spell/ritual** ●·······

_____

Statement of intention _____

_____

Moon Lunar Phase _____

Astrology/Planetary influences _____

_____

Weather _____

Materials or tools used/Ingredient/ Equipment

_____

_____

_____

Symbols used _____

Instructions _____

_____

Effective and feeling _____

_____

Immediate Changes and results _____

_____

Later changes and results _____

_____

Spell/Ritual rating _____

_____

_____

Date / Day of Week / Time

· · · • • • Name of spell/ritual • • • · ·

_____

Statement of intention _____

_____

Moon Lunar P-hase _____

Astrology/Planetary influences _____

_____

Weather _____

Materials or tools used/Ingredient/ Equipment

_____
_____
_____

Symbols used _____

Instructions _____

_____

Effective and feeling _____

_____

Immediate Changes and results _____

_____

Later changes and results _____

_____

Spell/Ritual rating _____

_____

_____

Date / Day of Week / Time

· · · · · ● **Name of spell/ritual** ● · · · · ·

_____

Statement of intention _____

_____

Moon Lunar P-base _____

Astrology/Planetary influences _____

_____

Weather _____

Materials or tools used/Ingredient/ Equipment

_____

_____

_____

Symbols used _____

Instructions _____

_____

Effective and feeling _____

_____

Immediate Changes and results _____

_____

Later changes and results _____

_____

Spell/Ritual rating _____

_____

_____

Date / Day of Week / Time

· · · · ● ● **Name of spell/ritual** ● ● ● · · ·

_____

Statement of intention _____

_____

Moon Lunar P-hase _____

Astrology/Planetary influences _____

_____

Weather _____

Materials or tools used/Ingredient/ Equipment

_____

_____

_____

Symbols used _____

Instructions _____

_____

Effective and feeling _____

_____

Immediate Changes and results _____

_____

Later changes and results _____

_____

Spell/Ritual rating _____

_____

_____

Date / Day of Week / Time

· · · · · ● **Name of spell/ritual** ● · · · · ·

_____

Statement of intention _____

_____

Moon Lunar Phase _____

Astrology/Planetary influences _____

_____

Weather _____

Materials or tools used/Ingredient/ Equipment

_____
_____
_____

Symbols used _____
Instructions _____

_____

Effective and feeling _____

_____

Immediate Changes and results _____

_____

Later changes and results _____

_____

Spell/Ritual rating _____

_____
_____

Date / Day of Week / Time

• • • • • Name of spell/ritual   • • • • • •

_____

Statement of intention   _____

_____

Moon Lunar Phase   _____

Astrology/Planetary influences   _____

_____

Weather   _____

Materials or tools used/Ingredient/ Equipment

_____
_____
_____

Symbols used   _____

Instructions   _____

_____

Effective and feeling   _____

_____

Immediate Changes and results   _____

_____

Later changes and results   _____

_____

Spell/Ritual rating   _____

_____

_____

Date / Day of Week / Time

• • • • • Name of spell/ritual • • • • • •

_____

Statement of intention _____

_____

Moon Lunar P-hase _____

Astrology/Planetary influences _____

_____

Weather _____

Materials or tools used/Ingredient/ Equipment

_____

_____

_____

Symbols used _____

Instructions _____

_____

Effective and feeling _____

_____

Immediate Changes and results _____

_____

Later changes and results _____

_____

Spell/Ritual rating _____

_____

_____

Date / Day of Week / Time

· · · · ● ● ● **Name of spell/ritual** ● ● ● · · · ·

_____

Statement of intention   _____

_____

Moon Lunar Phase   _____

Astrology/Planetary influences   _____

_____

Weather   _____

Materials or tools used/Ingredient/ Equipment

_____
_____
_____

Symbols used   _____

Instructions   _____

_____

Effective and feeling   _____

_____

Immediate Changes and results   _____

_____

Later changes and results   _____

_____

Spell/Ritual rating   _____

_____

_____

Date / Day of Week / Time

⋯•••• Name of spell/ritual •••• ⋯

Statement of intention _____

_____

Moon Lunar P–hase _____

Astrology/Planetary influences _____

_____

Weather _____

Materials or tools used/Ingredient/ Equipment

_____
_____
_____

Symbols used _____
Instructions _____

_____

Effective and feeling _____

_____

Immediate Changes and results _____

_____

Later changes and results _____

_____

Spell/Ritual rating _____

_____
_____

Date / Day of Week / Time

• • • • • Name of spell/ritual • • • • • •

_____

Statement of intention _____

_____

Moon Lunar P-hase _____

Astrology/Planetary influences _____

_____

Weather _____

Materials or tools used/Ingredient/ Equipment

_____

_____

_____

Symbols used _____

Instructions _____

_____

Effective and feeling _____

_____

Immediate Changes and results _____

_____

Later changes and results _____

_____

Spell/Ritual rating _____

_____

_____

Date / Day of Week / Time

・・・・・● Name of spell/ritual ●・・・・・・

_____

Statement of intention _____

_____

Moon Lunar P-hase _____

Astrology/Planetary influences _____

_____

Weather _____

Materials or tools used/Ingredient/ Equipment

_____

_____

_____

Symbols used _____

Instructions _____

_____

Effective and feeling _____

_____

Immediate Changes and results _____

_____

Later changes and results _____

_____

Spell/Ritual rating _____

_____

_____

Date / Day of Week / Time

• • • • Name of spell/ritual • • • • •

_____

Statement of intention _____

_____

Moon Lunar P-hase _____

Astrology/Planetary influences _____

_____

Weather _____

Materials or tools used/Ingredient/ Equipment

_____

_____

_____

Symbols used _____

Instructions _____

_____

Effective and feeling _____

_____

Immediate Changes and results _____

_____

Later changes and results _____

_____

Spell/Ritual rating _____

_____

_____

Date / Day of Week / Time

· · · · · · **Name of spell/ritual** · · · · · ·

_____

Statement of intention _____

_____

Moon Lunar P-hase _____

Astrology/Planetary influences _____

_____

Weather _____

Materials or tools used/Ingredient/ Equipment

_____

_____

_____

Symbols used _____

Instructions _____

_____

Effective and feeling _____

_____

Immediate Changes and results _____

_____

Later changes and results _____

_____

Spell/Ritual rating _____

_____

_____

Date / Day of Week / Time

· · · · ● ● **Name of spell/ritual** ● ● · · · ·

_____

Statement of intention _____

_____

Moon Lunar Phase _____

Astrology/Planetary influences _____

_____

Weather _____

Materials or tools used/Ingredient/ Equipment

_____
_____
_____

Symbols used _____

Instructions _____

_____

Effective and feeling _____

Immediate Changes and results _____

_____

Later changes and results _____

_____

Spell/Ritual rating _____

_____

_____

Date / Day of Week / Time

· · · · · ● **Name of spell/ritual** ● · · · · ·

_____

Statement of intention _____

_____

Moon Lunar P-hase _____

Astrology/Planetary influences _____

_____

Weather _____

Materials or tools used/Ingredient/ Equipment

_____

_____

_____

Symbols used _____

Instructions _____

_____

Effective and feeling _____

_____

Immediate Changes and results _____

_____

Later changes and results _____

_____

Spell/Ritual rating _____

_____

_____

Date / Day of Week / Time

• • • • ● **Name of spell/ritual** ● • • • • •

_____

Statement of intention _____

_____

Moon Lunar P-hase _____

Astrology/Planetary influences _____

_____

Weather _____

Materials or tools used/Ingredient/ Equipment

_____
_____
_____

Symbols used _____

Instructions _____

_____

Effective and feeling _____

_____

Immediate Changes and results _____

_____

Later changes and results _____

_____

Spell/Ritual rating _____

_____

_____

Date / Day of Week / Time

· · · · ● ● **Name of spell/ritual** ● ● ● · · ·

_____

Statement of intention _____

_____

Moon Lunar P-hase _____

Astrology/Planetary influences _____

_____

Weather _____

Materials or tools used/Ingredient/ Equipment

_____
_____
_____

Symbols used _____

Instructions _____

_____

Effective and feeling _____

_____

Immediate Changes and results _____

_____

Later changes and results _____

_____

Spell/Ritual rating _____

_____

_____

Date / Day of Week / Time

● ● ● ● ● **Name of spell/ritual** ● ● ● ● ● ●

_____

Statement of intention _____

_____

Moon Lunar P-hase _____

Astrology/Planetary influences _____

_____

Weather _____

Materials or tools used/Ingredient/ Equipment

_____

_____

_____

Symbols used _____

Instructions _____

_____

Effective and feeling _____

_____

Immediate Changes and results _____

_____

Later changes and results _____

_____

Spell/Ritual rating _____

_____

_____

Date / Day of Week / Time

· · · · ● ● **Name of spell/ritual** ● ● · · · ·

_____

Statement of intention _____

_____

Moon Lunar P-hase _____

Astrology/Planetary influences _____

_____

Weather _____

Materials or tools used/Ingredient/ Equipment

_____
_____
_____

Symbols used _____

Instructions _____

_____

Effective and feeling _____

_____

Immediate Changes and results _____

_____

Later changes and results _____

_____

Spell/Ritual rating _____

_____
_____

Date / Day of Week / Time

· · · • • • Name of spell/ritual • • • · ·

_____

Statement of intention _____

_____

Moon Lunar P-hase _____

Astrology/Planetary influences _____

_____

Weather _____

Materials or tools used/Ingredient/ Equipment

_____

_____

_____

Symbols used _____

Instructions _____

_____

Effective and feeling _____

_____

Immediate Changes and results _____

_____

Later changes and results _____

_____

Spell/Ritual rating _____

_____

_____

• • • • • Name of spell/ritual • • • • •

_____

Statement of intention _____

_____

Moon Lunar P-hase _____

Astrology/Planetary influences _____

_____

Weather _____

Materials or tools used/Ingredient/ Equipment

_____

_____

_____

Symbols used _____

Instructions _____

_____

Effective and feeling _____

_____

Immediate Changes and results _____

_____

Later changes and results _____

_____

Spell/Ritual rating _____

_____

_____

Date / Day of Week / Time

· · · ● ● ● **Name of spell/ritual** ● ● · · ·

_____

Statement of intention _____

_____

Moon Lunar Phase _____

Astrology/Planetary influences _____

_____

Weather _____

Materials or tools used/Ingredient/ Equipment

_____

_____

_____

Symbols used _____

Instructions _____

_____

Effective and feeling _____

_____

Immediate Changes and results _____

_____

Later changes and results _____

_____

Spell/Ritual rating _____

_____

_____

Date / Day of Week / Time

• • • • ● **Name of spell/ritual** ● • • • • •

_____

Statement of intention _____

_____

Moon Lunar P-hase _____

Astrology/Planetary influences _____

_____

Weather _____

Materials or tools used/Ingredient/ Equipment

_____

_____

_____

Symbols used _____

Instructions _____

_____

Effective and feeling _____

_____

Immediate Changes and results _____

_____

Later changes and results _____

_____

Spell/Ritual rating _____

_____

_____

Date / Day of Week / Time

• • • • • Name of spell/ritual • • • • •

_____

Statement of intention _____

_____

Moon Lunar P-hase _____

Astrology/Planetary influences _____

_____

Weather _____

Materials or tools used/Ingredient/ Equipment

_____

_____

_____

Symbols used _____

Instructions _____

_____

Effective and feeling _____

_____

Immediate Changes and results _____

_____

Later changes and results _____

_____

Spell/Ritual rating _____

_____

_____

Date / Day of Week / Time

· · · · · ● ● **Name of spell/ritual** ● ● · · · · ·

_____

Statement of intention _____

_____

Moon Lunar P-hase _____

Astrology/Planetary influences _____

_____

Weather _____

Materials or tools used/Ingredient/ Equipment

_____

_____

_____

Symbols used _____

Instructions _____

_____

Effective and feeling _____

_____

Immediate Changes and results _____

_____

Later changes and results _____

_____

Spell/Ritual rating _____

_____

_____

• • • • • Name of spell/ritual • • • • •

_____

Statement of intention _____

_____

Moon Lunar P-hase _____

Astrology/Planetary influences _____

_____

Weather _____

Materials or tools used/Ingredient/ Equipment

_____

_____

_____

Symbols used _____

Instructions _____

_____

Effective and feeling _____

_____

Immediate Changes and results _____

_____

Later changes and results _____

_____

Spell/Ritual rating _____

_____

_____

Date / Day of Week / Time

· · · · · ● **Name of spell/ritual** ● · · · · · ·

_____

Statement of intention _____

_____

Moon Lunar P-hase _____

Astrology/Planetary influences _____

_____

Weather _____

Materials or tools used/Ingredient/ Equipment

_____

_____

_____

Symbols used _____

Instructions _____

_____

Effective and feeling _____

_____

Immediate Changes and results _____

_____

Later changes and results _____

_____

Spell/Ritual rating _____

_____

_____

Date / Day of Week / Time

·····● Name of spell/ritual ●·····

_____

Statement of intention _____

_____

Moon Lunar P-hase _____

Astrology/Planetary influences _____

_____

Weather _____

Materials or tools used/Ingredient/ Equipment

_____

_____

_____

Symbols used _____

Instructions _____

_____

Effective and feeling _____

_____

Immediate Changes and results _____

_____

Later changes and results _____

_____

Spell/Ritual rating _____

_____

_____

Date / Day of Week / Time

• • • • • Name of spell/ritual • • • • • •

_____

Statement of intention _____

_____

Moon Lunar P–hase _____

Astrology/Planetary influences _____

_____

Weather _____

Materials or tools used/Ingredient/ Equipment

_____

_____

_____

Symbols used _____

Instructions _____

_____

Effective and feeling _____

_____

Immediate Changes and results _____

_____

Later changes and results _____

_____

Spell/Ritual rating _____

_____

_____

Date / Day of Week / Time

· · · · ● ● Name of spell/ritual ● ● · · · · ·

_____

Statement of intention _____

_____

Moon Lunar P-hase _____

Astrology/Planetary influences _____

_____

Weather _____

Materials or tools used/Ingredient/ Equipment

_____
_____
_____

Symbols used _____
Instructions _____

_____

Effective and feeling _____

_____

Immediate Changes and results _____

_____

Later changes and results _____

_____

Spell/Ritual rating _____

_____

_____

Date / Day of Week / Time

· · · · ● ● Name of spell/ritual ● ● · · · ·

_____

Statement of intention _____

_____

Moon Lunar P-hase _____

Astrology/Planetary influences _____

_____

Weather _____

Materials or tools used/Ingredient/ Equipment

_____

_____

_____

Symbols used _____

Instructions _____

_____

Effective and feeling _____

_____

Immediate Changes and results _____

_____

Later changes and results _____

_____

Spell/Ritual rating _____

_____

_____

Date / Day of Week / Time

· · · · ●● **Name of spell/ritual** ●● · · · ·

_____

Statement of intention _____

_____

Moon Lunar P-hase _____

Astrology/Planetary influences _____

_____

Weather _____

Materials or tools used/Ingredient/ Equipment

_____
_____
_____

Symbols used _____

Instructions _____

_____

Effective and feeling _____

_____

Immediate Changes and results _____

_____

Later changes and results _____

_____

Spell/Ritual rating _____

_____
_____

Date / Day of Week / Time

· · · · · ● **Name of spell/ritual** ● · · · · ·

_____

Statement of intention _____

_____

Moon Lunar P–hase _____

Astrology/Planetary influences _____

_____

Weather _____

Materials or tools used/Ingredient/ Equipment

_____

_____

_____

Symbols used _____

Instructions _____

_____

Effective and feeling _____

_____

Immediate Changes and results _____

_____

Later changes and results _____

_____

Spell/Ritual rating _____

_____

_____

Date / Day of Week / Time

• • • • • • Name of spell/ritual • • • • • •

_____

Statement of intention _____

_____

Moon Lunar P–hase _____

Astrology/Planetary influences _____

_____

Weather _____

Materials or tools used/Ingredient/ Equipment

_____

_____

_____

Symbols used _____

Instructions _____

_____

Effective and feeling _____

_____

Immediate Changes and results _____

_____

Later changes and results _____

_____

Spell/Ritual rating _____

_____

_____

Date / Day of Week / Time

· · · · • **Name of spell/ritual** • · · · · ·

_____

Statement of intention _____

_____

Moon Lunar P-hase _____

Astrology/Planetary influences _____

_____

Weather _____

Materials or tools used/Ingredient/ Equipment

_____
_____
_____

Symbols used _____

Instructions _____

_____

Effective and feeling _____

_____

Immediate Changes and results _____

_____

Later changes and results _____

_____

Spell/Ritual rating _____

_____

_____

Date / Day of Week / Time

• • • • • Name of spell/ritual • • • • •

_____

Statement of intention _____

_____

Moon Lunar Phase _____

Astrology/Planetary influences _____

_____

Weather _____

Materials or tools used/Ingredient/ Equipment

_____
_____
_____

Symbols used _____

Instructions _____

_____

Effective and feeling _____

_____

Immediate Changes and results _____

_____

Later changes and results _____

_____

Spell/Ritual rating _____

_____

_____

Date / Day of Week / Time

· · · · ● ● **Name of spell/ritual** ● ● ● · · ·

_____

Statement of intention _____

_____

Moon Lunar P-hase _____

Astrology/Planetary influences _____

_____

Weather _____

Materials or tools used/Ingredient/ Equipment

_____
_____
_____

Symbols used _____
Instructions _____

_____

Effective and feeling _____

_____

Immediate Changes and results _____

_____

Later changes and results _____

_____

Spell/Ritual rating _____

_____

_____

Date / Day of Week / Time

• • • • • Name of spell/ritual • • • • •

_____

Statement of intention _____

_____

Moon Lunar P-hase _____

Astrology/Planetary influences _____

_____

Weather _____

Materials or tools used/Ingredient/ Equipment

_____

_____

_____

Symbols used _____

Instructions _____

_____

Effective and feeling _____

_____

Immediate Changes and results _____

_____

Later changes and results _____

_____

Spell/Ritual rating _____

_____

_____

Date / Day of Week / Time

●●●●● **Name of spell/ritual** ●●●●●

_____

Statement of intention _____

_____

Moon Lunar P-hase _____

Astrology/Planetary influences _____

_____

Weather _____

Materials or tools used/Ingredient/ Equipment

_____
_____
_____

Symbols used _____

Instructions _____

_____

Effective and feeling _____

_____

Immediate Changes and results _____

_____

Later changes and results _____

_____

Spell/Ritual rating _____

_____
_____

Date / Day of Week / Time

·····●●● Name of spell/ritual ●●●·····

_____

Statement of intention _____

_____

Moon Lunar P-base _____

Astrology/Planetary influences _____

_____

Weather _____

Materials or tools used/Ingredient/ Equipment

_____

_____

_____

Symbols used _____

Instructions _____

_____

Effective and feeling _____

_____

Immediate Changes and results _____

_____

Later changes and results _____

_____

Spell/Ritual rating _____

_____

Date / Day of Week / Time

· · · · ● ● **Name of spell/ritual** ● ● ● · · ·

_____

Statement of intention _____

_____

Moon Lunar P-hase _____

Astrology/Planetary influences _____

_____

Weather _____

Materials or tools used/Ingredient/ Equipment

_____

_____

_____

Symbols used _____

Instructions _____

_____

Effective and feeling _____

_____

Immediate Changes and results _____

_____

Later changes and results _____

_____

Spell/Ritual rating _____

_____

_____

Date / Day of Week / Time

• • • • • Name of spell/ritual • • • • • •

_____

Statement of intention _____

_____

Moon Lunar P-hase _____

Astrology/Planetary influences _____

_____

Weather _____

Materials or tools used/Ingredient/ Equipment

_____

_____

_____

Symbols used _____

Instructions _____

_____

Effective and feeling _____

_____

Immediate Changes and results _____

_____

Later changes and results _____

_____

Spell/Ritual rating _____

_____

_____

Date / Day of Week / Time

· · · · · ● **Name of spell/ritual** ● · · · · · ·

_____

Statement of intention _____

_____

Moon Lunar Phase _____

Astrology/Planetary influences _____

_____

Weather _____

Materials or tools used/Ingredient/ Equipment

_____
_____
_____

Symbols used _____

Instructions _____

_____

Effective and feeling _____

_____

Immediate Changes and results _____

_____

Later changes and results _____

_____

Spell/Ritual rating _____

_____
_____

Date / Day of Week / Time

• • • • • ● Name of spell/ritual ● • • • • •

_____

Statement of intention _____

_____

Moon Lunar P-hase _____

Astrology/Planetary influences _____

_____

Weather _____

Materials or tools used/Ingredient/ Equipment

_____

_____

_____

Symbols used _____

Instructions _____

_____

Effective and feeling _____

_____

Immediate Changes and results _____

_____

Later changes and results _____

_____

Spell/Ritual rating _____

_____

_____

Date / Day of Week / Time

· · · · ● **Name of spell/ritual** ● ● · · · ·

_____

Statement of intention _____

_____

Moon Lunar P-hase _____

Astrology/Planetary influences _____

_____

Weather _____

Materials or tools used/Ingredient/ Equipment

_____

_____

_____

Symbols used _____

Instructions _____

_____

Effective and feeling _____

_____

Immediate Changes and results _____

_____

Later changes and results _____

_____

Spell/Ritual rating _____

_____

_____

Date   / Day of Week / Time

• • • • • Name of spell/ritual • • • • •

_____

Statement of intention   _____

_____

Moon Lunar P-hase   _____

Astrology/Planetary influences   _____

_____

Weather   _____

Materials or tools used/Ingredient/ Equipment

_____
_____
_____

Symbols used   _____

Instructions   _____

_____

Effective and feeling   _____

_____

Immediate Changes and results   _____

_____

Later changes and results   _____

_____

Spell/Ritual rating   _____

_____

_____

Date / Day of Week / Time

· · · · · ● ● **Name of spell/ritual** ● ● · · · · ·

_____

Statement of intention _____

_____

Moon Lunar P-hase _____

Astrology/Planetary influences _____

_____

Weather _____

Materials or tools used/Ingredient/ Equipment

_____

_____

_____

Symbols used _____

Instructions _____

_____

Effective and feeling _____

_____

Immediate Changes and results _____

_____

Later changes and results _____

_____

Spell/Ritual rating _____

_____

_____

Date / Day of Week / Time

• • • • • Name of spell/ritual • • • • •

_____

Statement of intention _____

_____

Moon Lunar Phase _____

Astrology/Planetary influences _____

_____

Weather _____

Materials or tools used/Ingredient/ Equipment

_____

_____

_____

Symbols used _____

Instructions _____

_____

Effective and feeling _____

_____

Immediate Changes and results _____

_____

Later changes and results _____

_____

Spell/Ritual rating _____

_____

_____

Date / Day of Week / Time

· · · · · ● **Name of spell/ritual** ● · · · · ·

_____

Statement of intention _____

_____

Moon Lunar P-hase _____

Astrology/Planetary influences _____

_____

Weather _____

Materials or tools used/Ingredient/ Equipment

_____

_____

_____

Symbols used _____

Instructions _____

_____

Effective and feeling _____

_____

Immediate Changes and results _____

_____

Later changes and results _____

_____

Spell/Ritual rating _____

_____

_____

Date / Day of Week / Time

• • • • ● Name of spell/ritual ● • • • • •

_____

Statement of intention _____

_____

Moon Lunar P-hase _____

Astrology/Planetary influences _____

_____

Weather _____

Materials or tools used/Ingredient/ Equipment

_____

_____

_____

Symbols used _____

Instructions _____

_____

Effective and feeling _____

_____

Immediate Changes and results _____

_____

Later changes and results _____

_____

Spell/Ritual rating _____

_____

_____

Date / Day of Week / Time

· · · · · ● **Name of spell/ritual** ● · · · · ·

_____

Statement of intention _____

_____

Moon Lunar P-hase _____

Astrology/Planetary influences _____

_____

Weather _____

Materials or tools used/Ingredient/ Equipment

_____

_____

_____

Symbols used _____

Instructions _____

_____

Effective and feeling _____

_____

Immediate Changes and results _____

_____

Later changes and results _____

_____

Spell/Ritual rating _____

_____

_____

Date / Day of Week / Time

· · · · · ● Name of spell/ritual ● · · · · ·

_____

Statement of intention _____

_____

Moon Lunar P-hase _____

Astrology/Planetary influences _____

_____

Weather _____

Materials or tools used/Ingredient/ Equipment

_____

_____

_____

Symbols used _____

Instructions _____

_____

Effective and feeling _____

_____

Immediate Changes and results _____

_____

Later changes and results _____

_____

Spell/Ritual rating _____

_____

_____

Date / Day of Week / Time

· · · · · ● ● **Name of spell/ritual** ● ● · · · ·

_____

Statement of intention _____

_____

Moon Lunar P-hase _____

Astrology/Planetary influences _____

_____

Weather _____

Materials or tools used/Ingredient/ Equipment

_____
_____
_____

Symbols used _____

Instructions _____

_____

Effective and feeling _____

_____

Immediate Changes and results _____

_____

Later changes and results _____

_____

Spell/Ritual rating _____

_____

_____

Date / Day of Week / Time

·····● Name of spell/ritual ●·····

_____

Statement of intention _____

_____

Moon Lunar Phase _____

Astrology/Planetary influences _____

_____

Weather _____

Materials or tools used/Ingredient/ Equipment

_____

_____

_____

Symbols used _____

Instructions _____

_____

Effective and feeling _____

_____

Immediate Changes and results _____

_____

Later changes and results _____

_____

Spell/Ritual rating _____

_____

_____